DISCERNMENT

Transforming Power in Daily Life

Workshop Manual

by
Nadine
Hoover

90 W. University St., Alfred, New York 14802
www.ConscienceStudio.com

Hoover, Nadine
Discernment; Transforming Power in Daily Life

ISBN 978-0-9828492-3-1

1. Peace & Nonviolence
2. Decision-making
2. Organizational Development

Cover Design: Terese Longva
Technical Support: Devin Henry

Printed by Lightning Source, USA, UK, Russia and Australia.

Dedicated to
Pamela Haines,
whose gracious attention
brought this into being.

Table of Contents

Note to Readers *vii*
Note to Facilitators *viii*
Acknowledgements *ix*

Workshop Routines

Sample Schedules 3
Sample Agenda 4
Session Openings 6
Agenda Previews 6
Light & Livelies 7
Session Reflections 7
Session Closings 7
Major Activities List 8
Materials List 9

Workshop Sessions

Session I: Community ***13***
Opening Talk 14
Cooperative Agreements 16
Affirmation Names 18
Picture Sharing: *Remember Transforming Power* 18
Journaling: *Commitment to Self* 21

Session II: Convincement ***23***
Gathering for Silence: *Stop & Open* 24
Visiting Self 26
Gathering for Sharing: *Conveying Transforming Power* 27
Journaling: *Experiences of Transforming Power* 29

Session III: Conviction *31*
Gathering for Silence: *Listen & Speak* 32
Good Companions 33
Visiting Companions: *Experiences in Hard Times* 36
Concentric Circles: *Effects of Prejudice and Privilege* 38

Session IV: Transformation *41*
Gathering for Silence: *Change & Write* 42
Web Brainstorming: *Awareness of Transforming Power* 43
Personal Transformation: *Experimenting* 44
Empathy: *Feedback* 45

Session V: Feedback *47*
Gathering for Silence: *Available & Prepared* 48
Fishbowl: *Feedback on Experimenting* 49
Visiting Companions: *Feedback* 52
Gathering for Feedback 54
Gathering for Discernment 55

Session VI: Wrap-up *57*
Whisper Circle 58
Personal Reflection 59
Affirmation Posters 60
Open Questions 60
Next Steps 60
Reflection of the Whole 61

Appendices

Moving *65*
Journaling *66*
Visiting *68*
Gathering *70*
Experimenting *72*
Shifting Approach *73*
Author's Note *75*
Bibliography *76*

Note to Readers

Discernment is *the ability to perceive and grasp the inward character and relationship of things, especially when obscure, leading to keen insight and judgment.* Discernment begins with individuals' personal practice, which then is tested with companions and with community, then tested with neighboring communities, then documented as guidance for individuals. This self-referential cycle works as a functioning whole.

Nadine Hoover developed this workshop in the format and approach of the Alternatives to Violence Project (AVP). After a prerequisite basic AVP workshop on transforming power, people who choose to practice nonviolence daily may participate in advanced special topic workshops. In this context discernment *is the practice of how to live aware of and in accord with transforming power in every moment.* The workshop is best facilitated by teams of three or more facilitators who actively practice discernment in daily life. We facilitate in order to enrich our own personal practice. Regular practice of these skills allows facilitators to demonstrate and explain with full richness and complexity. Changes in ourselves then naturally lead to changes in others. All participants are volunteers and none may be in a position of power over another—guards with those incarcerated, teachers with students, administrators with staff, etc. Family members are asked to consider whether or not to participate in the same workshop. A facilitator should speak independently with the youngest family member to ensure there is a real desire to participate without coercion.

The founders of AVP used consensus as a first step in which to gather with mutual respect and listen to one another. The standard second-level AVP workshop introduces consensus. These founders, however, made decisions based on their best sense of what was right and true, whereas consensus in the end must accommodate each individual voice, whether inspired or distressed. Discernment may be religious, spiritual, conscientious or ethical according to each person's belief, but the ecology of discernment practices is universal across time, location and belief. These practices have been the core of experiments in community and governance and is currently a viable, underutilized option for organizing and administering contemporary social structures.

Note to Facilitators

This workshop is for people who allow transforming power to shape and guide their daily life. In other words, this is an advanced workshop for people mutually committed to practicing peace and nonviolence and living in accord with their conscience within communities of conscience.

Schedule some time the day or week before the workshop to prepare materials and practice giving instructions. Team building then takes about three to four additional hours. Leave plenty of time to greet participants as they arrive. The facilitation team meets on breaks and immediately after the workshop to cover these topics: Check-in; Activities; Participants; Facilitator Feedback; Session Agendas (next two); and Team Affirmations.

At the start of the workshop, gather in silence, then offer an orientation to the land, noting local features and first peoples who cared for the land before us, how we care for the land today, the rhythm of the day and facilities available. Singing, introductions, learning names, get-to-know-each-other games and a light supper help people relax and become comfortable with one another.

The original recommendation for one session on prejudice and stereotyping proves persistently necessary. We need more activities on prejudice, oppression and privilege than the minimal Concentric Circle questions in this manual. A local AVP and/or sponsoring office may appreciate a written workshop report, including the number and names of facilitators and participants, date, time, place, schedule, agenda and any comments or learnings from the workshop.

Gatherings, Light & Livelies, self care and closings are selected by the facilitation team in relation to the needs of the group, the space available and the theme of the session. Specific timing and activities in this agenda are suggestions. Facilitators may be compensated to facilitate this workshop in part or in whole as an AVP-style workshop, but under a separate name. Being compensated, although valid, changes the fundamental nature of a workshop, take care to honestly realize any dependencies or conflicts of interest as well as supports that arise with compensation. If not under the name of AVP, a basic workshop equivalent is still expected before this work is undertaken.

Acknowledgements

Tremendous gratitude goes out to people close to me—my two daughters, Fenna Mandolang and Sarah Rozard, and son-in-law, Nicholas Rozard, who all in their own way cheer me on and tolerate my absences; my parents, Dean and Sharon Hoover, who asked, "Are you writing?" and my brother Mark Hoover, who is always there for me.

I am indebted to the peace, civil rights and women's rights activists who developed the Alternatives to Violence Project (AVP) in collaboration with men formerly incarcerated in Greenhaven prison who cared so deeply for youth in their communities. I do not know who I would be as a person without their contributions.

This book took of three years of development and two years of facilitating and writing. Many people encouraged me with their words, generosity and patience. Particularly Gay Howard, Diantha Horton and Pamela Haines, who paid attention, shared income and offered calm, balanced encouragement. I am also tremendously grateful to the numerous Quakers who supported me in their homes to write for extended periods between May 2010 to May 2012: Kathleen Gale; David Snaith, Donna Starr and Autumn and Katy Star; Steve, Bronwyn, Alma and Elsa Mohlke; and Pamela Haines and Chuck Esser. In May 2012, after two years, there were still no apparent results and I 'gave up.'

In June 2012, I arrived in Langsa, Aceh, under the care of Friends Peace Teams in Asia West Pacific. The Acehnese AVP facilitators announced, "You're delinquent! We've been doing AVP workshops for seven years and you've never offered the second-level workshop. It's time." The second-level AVP workshop on consensus, although a solid first step, falls short of the practice I experienced in the early AVP community and falls short of what is needed for organizations and people's movements around the globe. AVP founders used to make decisions, which proved fruitful for us all. In contrast, Occupy Wall Street groups in several major world cities called for advice because consensus and community distress tore them apart. I wanted to offer this ecology of practice in discernment, but had no language to explain it prepared or available to others. Because of this, I told the Acehnese I could not do the traditional workshop on consensus, but would try to do the best workshop I could on discernment with the understanding that I had worked on it for several years with mixed results.

Our Acehnese friends agreed to experiment on ourselves and we embarked together. They were the ones who also tried out and refined an AVP workshop on trauma healing. Once again, they provided the context to create an amazing new workshop! Aceh remains one of the most difficult places to function or accomplish work, yet has been one of the greatest contributors to the development of new workshops for practicing peace and nonviolence.

AVP-USA and AVP-International offered opportunities to share and refine the discernment workshop, including the pre-gathering workshop at AVP International Gathering 2015 in Ireland facilitated by Nadine Hoover, Petrus, Jamuna Shrestha and Kishor Rijal.

I could not have sustained the relationships in Aceh, North Sumatra and Central Java that led to this work if not for the persistent support of numerous people around the world who create and sustain Friends Peace Teams. Scores of people serving on the Friends Peace Teams governing Council and two dozen spiritual companions give me consistent attention and feedback.

I appreciate feedback and editing graciously offered by Sharon Hoover, Emily Westacott and Sarah Rozard, which greatly improved the clarity of the writing.

Finally I thank Jeanne Hyland, whose smile and laugh is the nourishment that keeps me oriented; she is a living testimony of my faith in the extraordinary power of the ordinary. She relates directly to everyone and the earth with love, inquisitiveness and generosity of spirit.

Workshop Routines

Sample Schedules

Sample Agenda

Session Openings

Agenda Previews

Light & Livelies

Session Reflections

Session Closings

Major Activities List

Materials List

Sample Schedules

An 18–21 hour schedule is typical for this workshop, because it takes time to create community, absorb new ideas, practice new behaviors, and be changed by the learning. Since these practices are new to most people, at some point people hit absorption capacity, regardless of the time available. Workshops in prison must be adjusted to the institution's constraints and in religious communities to prayer and worship schedules and in various locations to the time zones. If three days are available, a comfortable schedule might be:

Day 1	*9:00 – 4:30*	*7.5 hrs*	*Practice & Team Building*
Day 2–4	8:30 – 12:00	3.5 hrs	Sessions I, III, V
	1:00 – 4:30	3.5 hrs	Sessions II, IV, VI
Day 5	*6:00 – 9:00*	*3 hrs*	*Team Debriefing*
Total Time in Session:		**21 hrs**	

The morning session could be 8:30-noon or 9:00-12:30 with an hour or an hour and a half lunch followed by an afternoon session of 1:00-4:30 or 1:30-5:00, retaining 21 hrs. A comfortable weekend schedule might be:

Day 1	*9:00 – 4:00*	*7 hrs*	*Practice & Team Building*	
	6:30 – 9:30	3 hrs	Session I:	Community
Day 2	8:30 – 12:00	3.5 hrs	Session II:	Convincement
	1:00 – 5:00	4 hrs	Session III:	Conviction
	6:30 – 9:30	3 hrs	Session IV:	Transformation
Day 3	8:30 – 12:00	3.5 hrs	Session V:	Feedback
	1:00 – 4:00	3 hrs	Session VI:	Wrap-up
	5:00 – 8:00	*3 hrs*	*Team Debriefing*	
Total Time in Session:		**20 hrs**		

- When scheduling, do not plan Session III directly before bedtime or when an activity cannot be completed. Its activities delve into emotional personal material and should not be the activities with which to end the day.
- A residential workshop gives people time to interact outside sessions while we prepare food, cook and clean, as well as ensures consistent attendance.
- Protect time and space to rest. Ask each person both to help and to care for himself or herself. Encourage calmness, especially when eating.

Sample Agenda

Session I: Community
Opening: Name and *one thing I'm hoping for from this workshop is…*
Agenda Preview
Opening Talk
Cooperative Agreements
Affirmation Names *(with an active name game)*
Picture Sharing: *Remember Transforming Power*
Journaling: *Commitment to Self*
Reflection and Closing

Session II: Convincement
Gathering for Silence: *Stop & Open*
Opening: Name and *names I use for the source of life that is beyond naming…*
Agenda Preview
Light & Lively *(using names)*
Visiting Self
Gathering for Sharing: *Conveying Transforming Power*
Journaling: *Experiences of transforming power*
Light & Lively *(with affirmation)*
Reflection and Closing

Session III: Conviction
Gathering for Silence: *Listen & Speak*
Opening: Name and *a place that makes me really happy is…*
Agenda Preview
Good Companions
Visiting Companions: *How I experience transforming power in hard times is…*
Journaling: *Confidence in Transforming Power*
Light & Lively *(with movement and laughter)*
Concentric Circles: *Effects of prejudice and privilege…*
Reflection and Closing

Session IV: Transformation
Gathering for Silence: *Change & Write*
Opening: Name and *a sound that represents how I feel right now is... or how I feel as the weather report is...*
Agenda Preview
Web Brainstorming: *What I need to be aware of transforming power in every moment...*
Personal Transformation: *Experimenting with transforming power...*
Light & Lively
Empathy: *Feedback*
Journaling: *Experimenting with transforming power in daily life...*
Reflection and Closing

Session V: Feedback
Gathering for Silence: *Available and Prepared*
Opening: Name and *a person who loves me and why...*
Agenda Preview
Fishbowl: *Feedback on experimenting with transforming power*
Light & Lively *(with movement and laughter)*
Visiting Companions: *Feedback*
Gathering for Feedback *(often limited by energy and/or time)*
Journaling: *Being a good companion, listening to where words come from...*
Reflection and Closing

Session VI: Wrap-up
Gathering for Silence
Opening: Name and *one thing I'm taking home with me is...*
Agenda Preview
Whisper Circle or Personal Reflection
Light & Lively
Affirmation Posters
Open Questions
Next Steps
Reflection of the Whole and Closing

Session Openings

Facilitators think through a couple responses to the session opening prior to session so she may focus on the group rather than her answer. Start each session with participants sitting in a circle with no obstructions in the center, so everyone has a clear line of sight. Ideally, facilitators sit in the circle at least three minutes before the appointed time and make every effort to sit in different places next to different people at every opportunity. Facilitators do not sit next to one another. Begin each opening by going around the circle starting with yourself, each person responds to a stem sentence or question that fits with the group, theme of the session and time available.

Openings may be fast or slow depending on the topic, how the leader models the response and the number of people in the group. If the time is short or the group large, ask for and model a quick response. Participants will follow the facilitators' example in the length and depth of their response. Opening the session in this manner helps people transition from individual to group activities and continue to get to know one another. Openings offer the opportunity to practice speaking and listening as well as tangibly representing the distributed respect and power required for peace and nonviolence. *(5–25 minutes)*

Agenda Previews

Post the agenda for the session on the wall. At the beginning of each session, read the names of the activities, not the assigned facilitators, to maintain focus on the activities rather than the facilitators. Stand beside the agenda facing the group to draw everyone's eye and read the activities out loud without elaborating. It only takes a minute or two. The same person who does the opening may also read the agenda.

The agenda preview serves as an advanced organizer for everyone to share the power and information, gives participants a sense of where the session is going and supports visual learners. Although participants do not yet know the content of the activities, they often follow along to regulate their participation depending on how many activities are left on the agenda and the remaining time available. *(1-3 minutes)*

Light & Livelies

Light & Livelies keep people awake and moving, activate the cerebral cortex, discharge distress, bring people fully into the present and support kinesthetic learners. Light & Livelies help people relax and enjoy themselves, each other, the group and life! Typically schedule ten minutes, but one activity may take up to 30 minutes or more. Fit them with the session theme, group needs and time available. This workshop requires active Light & Livelies *(see AVP Manual).*

(10⁺ minutes)

Session Reflections

At the end of each session, reread the agenda item-by-item. For each activity give time for participants to recall the activity. Recount an example or unique moment from the activity to help bring the memory back to life, then ask: *What was this activity like for you? What happened for you in this activity? What did you notice?* Additional questions might be: *What did you get (or learn) from this? After doing this, what might you do differently when you go home? How do you see this related to transforming power or discernment in your life?* Record participant comments on a separate sheet of paper (we often reuse the agendas). Facilitators do not comment or respond during this reflection time, empowering participants to speak freely. Add questions to the Open Questions *(pp 15 & 60)* rather than respond to them at this time. Explain that this time is for their feedback, not for discussion. Allow time for participants to recall the activity and to say whatever comes to mind. Facilitators discuss participant feedback later in the team clinic. *(5–15 minutes)*

Session Closings

End each session with a brief activity such as a song, affirmation or activity that brings the group together. Closings honor the group, support transitions, affirm the work and affirm our commitment to take this work into our daily lives. *(5–10 minutes)*

Major Activities List

Session I: Community
Opening Talk
Cooperative Agreements
Affirmation Names
Picture Sharing: *Remember Transforming Power*
Journaling: *Commitment to Self*

Session II: Convincement
Gathering for Silence: *Stop & Open*
Visiting Self
Gathering for Sharing: *Conveying Transforming Power*
Journaling: *Experiences of Transforming Power*

Session III: Conviction
Gathering for Silence: *Listen & Speak*
Good Companions
Visiting Companions: *Experiences in Hard Times*
Concentric Circles: *Effects of Prejudice & Privilege*

Session IV: Transformation
Gathering for Silence: *Change & Write*
Web Brainstorming: *Awareness of Transforming Power*
Personal Transformation: *Experimenting*
Empathy: *Feedback*

Session V: Feedback
Gathering for Silence: *Available & Prepared*
Fishbowl: *Feedback on Experimenting*
Visiting Companions: *Feedback*
Gathering for Feedback

Session VI: Wrap-up
Whisper Circle or Personal Reflection
Open Questions & Next Steps
Reflection of the Whole

Materials List

Materials:
3-12 markers of 1-3 colors
30 flip chart sheets (fewer if using half sheets, if possible)
Masking tape
Handkerchiefs and/or tissues
Whiteboard or blackboard 48cm x 80cm; 18" x 24" (for fishbowl)
Whiteboard marker or chalk (for fishbowl)
Paper 7cm x 12cm; 3" x 5", one for each person (for empathy)
Pens or pencils for each person
Crayons (for affirmation posters)
Journal/blank book for each person
(fold a stack of 3-4 sheets of blank paper in half, staple a binding)
Transforming Power Mandala and Cards
Poster sheets (for affirmation posters)
Pictures (for picture sharing)
Supplies for prejudice exercises from the AVP Manual: Partial Knowledge (scenario), Dots (colored stickers), Masks (list of priorities)]

Posters:
AVP Principles
Purposes of this Workshop *(p 14)*
Roadmap & Open Questions *(p 15)*
Cooperative Agreements *(p 16)*
Collective Discernment: Things to Notice *(p 19)*
Examples of Commitments to Self *(p 21)*
Visiting Self (stem sentences in quadrants) *(p 26)*
Physical Discharge of Emotion & Good Companion *(pp 34-35)*
Visiting Companions & Questions for Visiting Companions *(pp 36-37)*
Integrity *(p 44)* & Available & Prepared *(p 48)*
Tests of Discernment *(p 53)*
Gatherings for Silence, Sharing, Feedback & Discernment *(pp 70-71)*
Next Steps *(contact information, upcoming events, steps for becoming a facilitator)*

***Resources** (additional resources listed in the Bibliography):*
Copies of **DISCERNMENT:** ***Transforming Power in Daily Life***

Workshop Sessions

Session I: Community

Session II: Convincement

Session III: Conviction

Session IV: Transformation

Session V: Feedback

Session VI: Wrap-Up

Session I

Community

Opening: Name and *one thing I'm hoping for from this workshop is…*

Agenda Preview

Opening Talk

Cooperative Agreements

Affirmation Names

Picture Sharing:
Remember Transforming Power

Journaling:
Commitment to Self

Reflection

Closing

Opening Talk

Keep the opening talk simple, direct and short, no more than ten minutes. Name the workshop, which is on discernment; do not elaborate. Begin by reading these simple Purposes of this Workshop:

> ### *Purposes of this Workshop*
>
> *Gain an understanding of discernment.*
> *Notice transforming power in all times, both easy and hard times.*
> *Practice basing daily decisions on discerning transforming power.*
> *Practice being a good companion to others.*

Explain that this is an advanced workshop for people who have chosen to live nonviolently and to let transforming power shape and guide their lives. This advanced workshop builds on the Alternatives to Violence Project (AVP) philosophy and approach of being open to transforming power, a palpable power available to each of us to change ourselves, others and situations for the better. Make a poster or describe the principles of AVP: it's an experiential workshop for personal change in which participants and facilitators volunteer both as teachers and learners, in which learning comes from combining experience and reflection to create insight rather than on experts or lectures and which is not religious, but may be inspirational. We will practice discernment in guiding decision-making, which requires investment in a healthy mind, heart and conscience. The activities in this workshop are drawn from:

1. ***Human Development:*** An understanding of how individuals, communities and societies develop, seek knowledge, cultivate insight, heal from trauma, discharge distress, experience joy and express conscience in daily life.

2. ***Quaker Practice:*** A practice of integrity in daily life, recorded over centuries, being both critical and creative in order to perceive, name and act in accord with the inward qualities and relationships of things.

3. ***Re-evaluation Counseling:*** A worldwide, voluntary, peer network of co-counselors who have developed a deep understanding of health, equality and overcoming oppression.

4. ***Alternatives to Violence Project (AVP):*** A practice of nonviolence in prisons and communities around the world, which is spread by alumni, who, over decades, share these activities with others because the practice has become important in their own lives.

Describe how the steps in the Road Map build on one another. When one is not working, go back and work on an earlier one, then return.

Road Map

Community Trust	—	*Principled Friendship*
Affirmation	—	*Safety*
Communication	—	*Remembering*
Cooperation	—	*Reconnection*
Convincement	—	*Conviction*
Transformation	—	*Feedback*
Direction	—	*Resolution of Disputes*

Cover basic supports for the workshop, such as:

1. Post an ***Open Questions*** poster on the wall for anyone to write questions as they arise, which will be revisited at the end of the workshop to ensure that all questions are addressed before closing.
2. Distribute journals. One may begin with an Open Questions page in the journal. Journals are private and will not be shared.
3. Ask the facilitators first, then the group, for permission to take photos or video prior to using the camera or recorder. Send copies of photos with captions including names and location to interested parties.
4. Decide who will write a report for the workshop and to whom it will be submitted. AVP-I or AVP Area Council would appreciate reports. A participant or a team member may volunteer.
5. Explain the logistics so everyone is comfortable while attending: bathrooms, phones, meals, sleeping arrangements, clean-up, etc.
6. Does anyone have anything to add? Any questions?

(10–15 minutes)

Cooperative Agreements

A sense of community is built by getting to know and affirm one another as well as setting safe boundaries through agreements. Some of the worst violence in the world is perpetrated among loved ones, friends and neighbors. Making explicit agreements shares power, but also raises concerns of what happens if agreements are broken and who will enforce them. Let the truth of an agreement exert its own power and let consequences be natural, not artificial, imposed or enforced. Agreements are flexible. As we practice, we look for the fewest agreements necessary in order to coordinate living, working and playing together peacefully. Post these agreements on the wall. Read and discuss each, one at a time. It is natural for the group to test and negotiate power at this juncture and important to give all the time participants need, usually 20–40 minutes, but maybe more. Make sure each agreement is understood and everyone has a chance to ask questions. After you verify that each is understood, ask if everyone agrees to practice them:

Cooperative Agreements

Respect and affirm self and others; no put downs.

Listen, don't interrupt.

Speak simply and honestly, without fear of mistakes.

Be authentic and changed by learning.

Make friends with people very different from oneself.

Include all 'sides,' there are no enemies.

Play regularly with young people and adults.

Discharge distress; speak directly to someone in dispute.

Ask for and give feedback and help.

Use what's needed and share the rest.

Tell one's own stories, not others'.

Use one's rights to pass, to consult, and to maintain privacy.

Volunteer oneself only, not others.

Value and care for each person, group, community and the land.

Live in integrity with the transforming power of life.

Unless there is a reason not to, write suggested changes on the poster. Explain that mistakes in practice are normal; it's the practice that matters. Ask each participant to notice if and when the agreements are broken and to remind one another to practice them. We let the group know that in our experience we can live peacefully and nonviolently when we all share a commitment to practice these agreements.

Post a blank poster underneath the agreements. Ask if any other guidelines are needed for us to feel safe and do our best work. Write down people's words without changing, improving or interpreting them. After three or more participants have spoken, facilitators may add items, such as:

- Attend all sessions; let the whole group know if you will be absent.
- Make decisions together about agenda times & returns from absence.
- Turn cell phones to silent or off; respond to cell messages on breaks.
- Be on time; sit in the circle before the appointed hour.
- Say your affirmation name, both adjective and given name, before speaking.
- Volunteer for food preparation and clean up.
- No smoking during sessions or inside the workshop space.
- Refrain from mood altering substances: caffeine, sugar, drugs, etc.
- Break for religious services; specify times.
- Use hand signals: note which ones…
- No side discussions in the large group.
- Be sure to sleep, so we are all rested for the next day.
- Tell a facilitator if you need to leave the room for a moment.

Use the language of each agreement as frequently as possible. Point out concrete examples of when and how the agreements are functioning as well as when and how they are violated. Draw people's attention back to the agreements regularly inside and outside workshop sessions.

We typically do not reflect in the large group after the Cooperative Agreement, but you may, especially if the group invests in these agreements. If time permits or is prioritized for this, ask participants to write the cooperative agreements in their journal along with any notes that seem significant to practicing these agreements here in the workshop as well as in daily life, such as which ones are particularly hard, easy or meaningful.

(20-40 minutes)

Affirmation Names

Affirmation opens a door to transforming power. The vocabulary of people exposed to prolonged violence drops to a fraction of the vocabulary of people living in peaceful circumstances and is almost entirely comprised of negative words. Using and hearing positive words, especially associated with our own person, is a strong contradiction to negative language and messages heard either as a child or later in life. Brainstorm positive adjectives that start with the same sound as each person's first name. Give each person time to pick one. If someone isn't sure or wishes to change adjectives, see how many positive words the group can brainstorm. Play with adjective names using movements or gestures. Describe what the adjectives mean. Play *Here I Sit* or *Blanket Game.* Ask if anyone in the group can say everyone's adjective and name in the group. Let everyone try who volunteers to do so. Laugh a lot and help each other. Say one's own name and adjective before speaking in the group. *(15–30 minutes)*

Picture Sharing

Remember Transforming Power

The approach to selecting images in this exercise helps people notice the quality and value of listening and mutual exploration, rather than the point of decision alone. Making decisions based on one's best sense of what is right and true requires resonance among people and with the environment. In other words, discernment needs to fit within the time and place as well as be 'correct.' Whereas bureaucratic society values the decision, discerning society values the mutual exploration and insights leading up to the decision. This whole process takes about one hour. Lay out on the floor a variety of pictures that may represent transforming power. We often cut pictures from magazines and try to get a range of dramatic, ordinary, colorful/black and white, large/small, young/old and so forth. Then take the following steps, being careful that the instructions remind participants that the goal is noticing the experience and stories of selecting, not the picture selected. Ask participants to:

1. Select one picture that represents transforming power to him or her personally and consider why.
2. Form a pair and take turns explaining how the picture represents transforming power, while the other person practices listening actively and attentively. Switch roles after three minutes when the facilitators says to do so and take a final minute for reflection or questions in the pair.
3. Take a moment to stand, stretch, breathe, change seats, move, etc.
4. As a pair, select one picture that best represents transforming power to the pair, rather than the individuals. Talk about why, forming one story as a pair, while noticing:

Collective Discernment: Things to Notice

- *Differences between the chose picture and the reason or story of why.*
- *Differences between selecting among stories or forming a group identity to select a picture and story that represents us.*
- *Differences between giving credit to the originator of a story and formulating one voice that represents or reflects the group as a whole.*
- *The group choice does not change the choice I made for myself.*
- *Any feelings of loss, gain, loneliness, camaraderie, fear, sadness, competition, excitement, delight or other feelings.*
- *Whether or not I use silence and inquiry as useful tools when feelings rise or ignore feelings and reinforce my arguments.*
- *Whether or not I listen in order to understand and consider before speaking, or in order to wait for my turn to repeat my story and position.*
- *Whether or not I interrupt.*
- *If we explore and play off each others' ideas to create a new story belonging to both of us or simply select one person's story.*

5. Discuss what choosing felt like, the balance between speaking and listening, the differences between personal and collective experiences of choosing, and the experience of creating a story together.
6. If time allows, select another pair to form a group of four and repeat the process: sharing, exchanging comments or questions, taking a break, beginning anew to discern and form a new, joint story.

In the large group, have each group discuss their group's process in light of the Collective Discernment: Things to Notice poster (p 19).

Notice how the language reveals if a group selected or pieced together separate stories that they all could agree to or if they got to know one another enough to form a group identity from which they could select a picture that represented them.

For reflection, ask: *What happened for you in this activity? What was that like for you?* You may add: *What did you get (or learn) from this? What will you do differently after this experience? What did you learn about transforming power in your life and community?*

(60 minutes)

Journaling

Commitment to Self

Keeping a journal or a log is a critical part of a sound experiment. What you write in your journal will not be shared. Yet the quality of one's journal is noticeable in one's work with others. Ask everyone to take ten minutes to write a commitment to oneself. Post examples, but ask people to formulate it in their own words, e.g.:

Examples of Commitments to Self

- *To stay aware of and experiment with transforming power in my life by making decisions based on my best discernment of what rings true.*
- *To experience the power of the Living Spirit that speaks to my human condition, in easy and hard times, and choose to let that Spirit shape and guide my life.*
- *To notice the goodness and capabilities in myself, others and life, ask for good attention, discharge pain and distress and reemerge with a clear heart and mind to live a full and beautiful life.*

The practices in this workshop come to life when backed by personal commitment, expressed through our words, will and motivation. Invite anyone who wishes to do so to write commitments on a large sheet and post it on the wall. *(See appendix for other journal topics.)*

(10–15 minutes)

Session II

Convincement

Gathering for Silence: *Stop & Open*

Opening: Name and *names I use for the source of life that is beyond naming... (or a song I like & why...)*

Agenda Preview

Light and Lively *(using names)*

Visiting Self

Gathering for Sharing:
Conveying Transforming Power

Journaling:
Experiences of Transforming Power

Light & Lively *(with affirmation)*

Reflection

Closing

Gathering for Silence
Stop & Open

When inwardly guided by conscience or one's best sense of life's transforming power, the line between being inspired and neurotic may be thin. What distinguishes them are whether or not we are able to stop and respond to external feedback, hence the central practices of sitting in silence and of giving and receiving feedback. In addition, learning to listen to that which is beyond words, behind the words or where the words come from is critical to discernment.

Discernment is "grasping the inward character and relationship among things." As a piano is tuned by the resonance in the silence around the notes, the inward character and relationship among things is sensed by the resonance in the silence within the moment or situation. Silence also provides the time and space to allow knowledge to absorb into one's being, including the fact that life is good and enough; nothing you can say or do will make you any better or more valuable than you are right now. Post on the wall:

Gathering for Silence

Stop • Open • Listen • Speak • Change • Write

- ***Stop****, sit silently and let yourself fall away. Let what you want, like or understand fall away.*
- ***Open*** *to transforming power. Value all life, the source of your breath and the source of your heart beat.*

This is enough*; nothing you can say or do will make you any more valuable than you are right now.*

- ***Listen*** *for truths working in you, listen to your conscience.*
- ***Speak****, simply and briefly, if there are implications for others.*
- ***Change*** *by yielding to the implications for your own life.*
- ***Write*** *implications for your life or community in your journal.*

- ***Leave silence*** *between speakers; speak only once, if at all.*

Gather as a group. Sit in a circle. Settle into the silence. The facilitator fully engages in the practice while also noticing the quality of the group. People who see this time as empty have trouble honoring it. Challenge people who make excuses to do other things at this time as a way to distract or avoid this work. The quality of the silence matters, so do everything you can to help people feel comfortable in the space, in the chairs, with the group and with the activity. Remind people of the critical nature of stopping, …of this is enough, …of knowing what to do in the silence, …of getting to know and feel the substance of the silence.

After three or more minutes of settling into the silence, state the first three points on the poster in a soft, even voice with long pauses between words or phrases.

Stop, */ sit silently and let yourself fall away. /*
Let what you want, like or understand / fall away. /

Open *to transforming power / and value all life; /*
the source of your breath, / and the source of your heart beat. /

This is enough; */ nothing you can say or do /*
will make you any more valuable / than you are right now. /

Stay in silence for at least 10–15 minutes, preferably 20 minutes as that is typically what it takes to truly 'stop', but the number of activities in the scheduled time probably does not permit this. Come out of silence with a few words, such as: "*Thank you, friends.*" Then greet people around you by holding the hands of the person on either side of you or shaking hands with those around you.

For reflection, ask: *What happened for you in this activity? What was that like for you?* At this stage, that is probably enough, although you may add questions such as, *What did you get (or learn) from that? What will you take from this into your daily life? How do you see this related to transforming power or discernment?*

(10–25 minutes)

Visiting Self

Discernment requires a capacity to know oneself and listen inwardly. As we do so, we cultivate a language of the inner landscape and encounter our conscience. Conscience is an inward knowledge of right and wrong with a compulsion to do what is right.

Listening inwardly requires vigilant care, mindfulness and honesty, with oneself and others, to distinguish among the variety of voices—egotistical, imposed, distressed, tempted, protectionist, disarmed, unencumbered, uninhibited, original, 'true'—while avoiding the pitfalls of both self-indulgence and self-denial.

Give each person a large sheet of paper (approximately 45cm x 30cm; 18" x 12") with a horizontal and vertical line through the center of the page, dividing the page into four quadrants. Post an example with the stem sentences at the top of each quadrant on landscaped paper:

My 'true self' is most apparent when…	*My 'true self' is least apparent when…*
Things others do that most bring out my 'true self' are…	*Things I do that most bring out others' 'true selves' are…*

When all the sentences are complete, have each person tape the paper to his or her chest and walk around reading each other's silently. Then tape the papers on the wall and return to the circle to look at all of them together. Reflect on this activity *(see page 7 for questions)*. Suggest to people that they might wish to copy this into their journals to reflect on later.

(45–60 minutes)

Gathering for Sharing
Conveying Transforming Power

To use discernment well, we must commit to both stopping regularly and to exchanging feedback. The latter relies on our ability to articulate our best sense of the presence and movement of transforming power and of what is loving and true in a moment or a situation.

A Native American once spoke about his conscience saying, "You'd have to ask my family, friends and neighbors," because a person's conscience becomes visible in his or her relationships to others and to the earth. Both the manifestation of conscience in daily life and discernment grow clearer, fuller and stronger with our ability to communicate. In a Gathering for Sharing, everyone has the opportunity to practice formulating language and speaking publicly from an inward place of insight and transforming power.

Gather in a circle as a group. Tell the group that this gathering will last 40 minutes to an hour and a quarter, depending on participation. Read these instructions, pointing to where they are posted on the wall:

Gathering for Sharing

Question • Advice • Direction • Dispute

- ***Gather*** *in silence and open to transforming power.*

Once quiet and open, then the convenor:

- ***Reads*** *a question, advice, direction or dispute to the group.*
- ***Asks*** *"Is it clear?" and clarifies as needed.*

Once clear, then:

- ***Speak*** *from one's conscience or best sense of what is true.*
- ***Leave silence*** *between speakers, giving everyone a chance to speak once before speaking again.*
- ***Listen*** *with empathy, open to becoming personally changed.*

Once insights or themes emerge (repeating with no new ideas):

- ***Speak*** *again of one's sense of the group as a whole.*
- ***Record*** *collective insights or implications for later feedback.*

Gathering for Sharing focuses all community members on one topic at a time. Any community member may suggest a topic, typically a genuine question of concern, suggested advice, direction sought for collective action or unsettled dispute. Take time to put the topic in writing. We learn a great deal about a subject when we try to formulate it into writing. Once the writing clearly represents our intention, then distribute or post it prior to the gathering.

In this workshop, tell the group that we will practice the Gathering for Sharing by all speaking to the question posted on the wall:

How do I experience transforming power in my daily life?

Settle into silence for a few minutes, typically 5-10 minutes. Then, in a soft but clear and even voice, read the question. Ask if this is clear. If not, clarify as briefly as possible. Once clear, invite people to speak from the silence when they feel ready. The convenor may keep mental note of who has not spoken. When it feels like the sharing or the time is coming to an end, say: "In a few minutes we will close, so if you haven't spoken yet, this would be a good time to speak." Then be quiet and leave time for any final speaking.

When closing, invite people to take a few notes briefly in their journals, if appropriate. After reflecting as a group, we advise each person to take as much time as needed to record insights or directions in one's journal.

A group or community who chooses to practice discernment may hold a Gathering for Sharing on a particular topic once, repeatedly until everyone gets to know one another on the topic, or on an ongoing basis. For instance, a group might meet weekly to share experiences of experimenting with discernment and transforming power in daily life. If the group meets a few times on a topic to inform a significant decision, when the group feels it is 'done', gather one last time on the topic. Often a surprising new level of sharing or insight occurs in such meetings. Usually 75–80 minutes is perfect, but group sharing may be done for any length of time, typically 20–180 minutes.

(60 -90 minutes)

Journaling
Experiences of Transforming Power

Public life in a post-nuclear age has been dominated by the myth that human destructiveness (and human industry) is greater than the creative, generative and regenerative power of life itself.

The message of 'nuclear winter' is that "we can wipe out all life as we know it," yet in reality life grows back, again and again. In order to place one's confidence in nonviolence, conscience and discernment, one has to get in touch with the magnitude of life's power. Persistently seeking a palpable sense of this power in our daily lives becomes pivotal to confidence and conviction.

In the journal, invite people to begin by writing about experiences of transforming power in daily life. Remind them that what they write in their journals will not be shared. Since they will write only for themselves, they are free to write on whatever seems most important. Spending some time on the specified topic, however, would be useful.

Ask everyone to take ten minutes to write how he or she experiences transforming power in daily life, moment to moment.

If anyone encounters a significant insight that might be true for others, invite them to consider writing it on the board or posting it on the wall. The writer may or may not sign it. If the writer signs the statement, it may become material for testing and feedback later in the workshop. *(See appendix for a further range of journal topics.)*

(10–15 minutes)

Session III
Conviction

Gathering for Silence: *Listen & Speak*

Opening: *Name and*
a place that makes me really happy is....

Agenda Preview

Good Companions

Visiting Companions:
How I experience transforming power
in hard times is...

Journaling:
Confidence in transforming power

Light & Lively
(with movement and laughter)

Concentric Circles:
Effects of prejudice and privilege...

Reflection

Closing

Gathering for Silence
Listen & Speak

Gather as a group sitting in a circle. Settle into the silence. After three or more minutes, read the first three points on the poster in a soft, even voice as a reminder:

- ***Stop,*** *sit silently and let yourself fall away. Let what you want, like or understand fall away.*
- ***Open*** *to transforming power. Value all life, the source of your breath and the source of your heart beat.*
- ***This is enough;*** *nothing you can say or do will make you any more valuable than you are right now.*

Then continue to read the next two points with long pauses. Pace your reading by attempting to hear and absorb the points yourself.

- ***Listen*** *for truths working in you, listen to your conscience.*
- ***Speak****, simply and briefly, if there are implications for others.*
- ***Leave silence*** between speakers; speak only once, if at all.

Stay in silence for at least 10–15 minutes, preferably 20 minutes as that is typically what it takes to truly 'stop.' Come out of silence with a few words, such as: "*Thank you, friends.*" Then greet people around you by holding the hands of the persons on either side of you or shaking hands with them. Ask if there are any thoughts that arose in the silence that anyone would like to share now. Give people a few minutes if anyone offers to speak. Remind people that they may speak in the silence if they feel the words may be important to others.

Close with some group reflection on the activity *(see page 7). Can you feel how active this work is, even though it is silent work? Can you feel how much time it takes to do this work? Can you feel how insights are sometimes for yourself and sometimes for us as a people?* Remind people to take notes in their journal. Tell participants that it is better to sit with the journal a moment and to see whether or not writing comes than to assume there is nothing to write.

(10–15 minutes)

Good Companions

Discernment is the ability to perceive and grasp the inner character and relationship of things, especially when obscure, leading to keen insight and judgment. Perception and comprehension emerge and strengthen as we are emotionally, mentally and spiritually clear and well. From childhood we face pains, defeats, oppressions and tragedies. These may cause lasting distress, particularly if we do not receive attention that affirms that we are good and capable in the moment of pain or injustice.

We know historic pains and distresses can lodge in the body, creating many forms of distortion, avoidance and triggering, if not released. The challenge is to release them and to let them go from the body, not just to relive or reenact them, ingraining them deeper into the body. Cultural inhibitions deny many natural, bodily healing processes such as crying, sobbing, shaking, stomping, yawning, and so forth. Although this inhibits release, it also protects from reliving or reenacting. We forfeit getting well in an attempt not to get worse.

When we commit to discernment, however, we need to commit to being as well as we can, learn to remember and release distresses and employ the clear mind that results. Being well requires that one:

1. Learn about primary emotions and how to discharge them.
2. Find another person with whom to practice good companionship, sharing time equally for emotional discharge, sharing and feedback.
3. Balance your attention as a companion to the past and present, the inside and outside of the body and the differences between fact and feeling.
4. Determine the length of time and stick with it. Learn that you can access memories, discharge distress and return to the present time.

Ask everyone to find a partner and a place in the room that is comfortable. Decide who will remember first; the other person is the companion. Ask the person remembering to take five minutes to remember something distressing. For this first session only, while remembering, please do not speak so that you may turn your attention to how the body wants to let go of the emotion. Read the ***Physical Discharge of Emotion*** poster (p 34).

Physical Discharge of Emotion

Emotional Stress		*Physical Release*
Grief	⇨	*Tears, crying, sobbing*
Fears	⇨	*Trembling, shivering, cold sweat, urinating, laughing*
Angers	⇨	*Angry noise, violent movement, warm sweat, laughing*
Boredom	⇨	*Non-repetitive conversing, laughing*
Physical Pains/Tension	⇨	*Yawning, stretching, scratching*

Discharge is the natural healing, not the pain.
Release and let go; do not hold on or relive.
Return to the present time and place with good attention.

see rc.org

Ask the companion to practice being a good companion. Note that the task of maintaining this level of attention and good intention is not easy and takes practice. If you drift while serving as a companion, just silently notice and bring your attention back to the task at hand.

Concentration improves with practice. Read the Good Companion poster.

Both roles may use speaking, but the primary focus of both is nonverbal. Therefore, in this introductory activity we ask that everyone practice both roles in silence. In future companion sessions, people typically will speak, but not necessarily and often sparingly. The use of silence is common, encouraged, respected and often quite fruitful. Therefore the guidelines refer to speaking, but we will practice at this time without speaking.

Good Companion

- *Pay attention with complete confidence in the goodness and capacity of the other and life's transforming power.*
- *Listen from the heart with relaxed, non-anxious attention.*
- *Breathe, stay calm, stay present and stay outside yourself. Emotion is contagious; resist picking up the other's emotions.*
- *Remember that loss of language and avoidance is natural and trust the other to select what to work on.*
- *Ask questions to show interest and encourage speaking and discharge, without pushing for a response.*
- *Keep time and maintain turns of equal time.*

DO NOT

Let the other person's problems bother you!!!

Cut someone off or pursue your own curiosity.

Tell similar stories or problems.

Give advice, direction or answers.

Steal the other's emotions.

Tell people to begin and go until you say to stop. In two or three minutes, in a soft, gentle voice remind everyone of the task of each role: *Notice how the body wants to let go. Don't hold onto the feeling, let it go. Companions relax. Notice the goodness and capability of your friend.* At about 4.5 minutes, ask the group to begin wrapping up and coming back. At about five minutes, ask everyone to come back and stand up, change their positions and do a grounding activity to bring them back to present time. Then ask them to move around a bit before changing seats. After the first round, the partners switch roles. After the second round, give the partners a minute or two to reflect on what it was like to do this in their pair. Return to the big group to reflect on the experience.

(40–50 minutes)

Visiting Companions
Experiences in Hard Times

Explain that companion groups typically meet regularly over time. The routine of the meetings matters more than the frequency or length of time. Most pairs meet every week or every two, four or six weeks. Some people prefer working in pairs, others in small groups of three or four. Five or six people is possible, but discouraged as a practice and not used in the workshop. When you get together, split the time equally, whether that is five, fifteen, thirty or sixty minutes each, with a little time at the beginning and end to settle in. If there is a pair or small group who might continue meeting after this workshop, they may use this opportunity to begin their practice here in the workshop.

Ask everyone to stand. Then ask everyone who wants to work in pairs to go to one side of the room and everyone who wants to work in small groups to go to the other side of the room. Ask people to form groups or pairs and find a comfortable place to sit in the room. Read the Visiting Companions poster:

Visiting Companions

- *2-4 people meet routinely (every 1-6 weeks) for 1-3 hours.*
- *Open with 5-10 minutes of silence.*
- *Share available time, taking equal turns.*
- *Pay attention as a good companion to encourage discharge and speaking.*
- *Ask questions that show interest or may help, NOT for discussion, to fill silence or to pursue your own curiosity.*
- *If asked, repeat what you heard as closely as possible in the speaker's words, without changing, improving or interpreting.*
- *Close with 5-10 minutes of silence.*

Let the group know how much time they have for the whole activity, count ten minutes to begin and end and divide up the remaining time among the number of group members. Ask the group to decide who will keep time on each person's turn. During a person's turn, do not interrupt. The person may be silent, may release emotion without speaking, may speak, or any combination. If they appear to look uncomfortable in the silence, just give them a moment to settle in. Do not try to rescue people from themselves. Silence is time to think, not a time to intervene.

Usually members of the group are invited to work on any of the Questions for Visiting Companions posted, but for this workshop everyone is asked to address the same question:

How I experience transforming power in the hard times, when I'm broken, am inadequate, have fallen short or have become the perpetrator, is...

Let people know that they will have ten to fifteen minutes at the end of the activity to journal about their trust or confidence in transforming power in every moment. Reflect in the large group.

Questions for Visiting Companions

- *How do I experience transforming power in both the easy and hard times?*
- *What distresses or rigid patterns do I need to discharge?*
- *What do I need to have or let go of in order to stay aware of transforming power in every moment?*
- *What truth is working in me? What are the implications?*
- *What am I learning from transforming power?...is it for others?*
- *How is truth prospering in my life? What are the fruits of my experiment, such as: love, joy, peace, strength, compassion, beauty, truth, equality, liberty and so forth?*
- *How can I ask for help, from whom, and what do I need?*
- *What is a good way to share the extra that I have and with whom?*

(45–60 minutes)

Concentric Circles
Effects of Prejudice & Privilege

Conviction emerges from the experience of transforming power in times when we are convicted, feel broken or inadequate, have fallen short or have become the perpetrator. At these times, we are able to see past our own ego to the great expanse and transforming power of abundant life upon which we can and do rely.

Human distresses, however, arise from personal, idiosyncratic experiences as well as from intergenerational patterns of distress: stereotyping, prejudice, oppression and privilege.

When we discern, we grasp the inner character and relationship of things, which requires curiosity in how personal and social distresses divide and affect us all. For example, *privilege is taking advantage of special benefits denied others, available because of inequality in power or control, at the detriment of others and/or the land.* Rather than believe that we 'earn' what we have, we must be willing to look at the whole social fabric that creates the conditions of advantage and disadvantage that allows or restricts us from having what we want.

In facing, rather than avoiding or denying these dynamics, we may acknowledge how unjust balances of power shape our situations and consider what life would be like without them. People who benefit from imbalances of power tend to prefer to ignore and/or discount the affect on their life, while people who suffer from imbalances of power cannot ignore the intruding nature of its effect. Noticing and talking about this begins to break down these patterns, releasing whole new experiences of transforming power in our daily lives.

Ask every other person to come into the circle and turn and face the person to their left, forming an inside circle facing out and an outside circle facing in. Explain that the facilitator will read a topic and give everyone a few moments to think about their response. Then, the outside circle will begin speaking on a topic for about three minutes. The facilitator will tell you when to switch. Then the inside circle will speak for three minutes. After both persons get three minutes to speak, one of the circles stands and moves one person to the right and repeats the process until all the participants have spoken to all the topics. You may alternate which circle responds first and which circle stands and rotates.

Suggested topics are:

- *A rigid decision I made as a child when I was hurt or ignored that has stayed with me and affects the way I respond when I'm stressed was…*
- *Ways authority or control are exercised unjustly in our society are…*
- *How the unjust exercise of authority or control affects my life…*
- *What society would be like if it were just is…*

The facilitation team may choose these or other topics, remembering to select topics that will bring to light how privilege and oppression affect all our lives.

Ask one circle to rotate to the left between each topic, alternating between the inside and outside circles. Also alternate between the inside and outside circles which circle begins to speak first. Reflect in the large group.

(7 minutes/topic + 20 minutes instruction and reflection)

Session IV

Transformation

Gathering for Silence: *Change & Write*

Opening: *Name and a sound that represents how I feel right now is… or how I feel as the weather report is…*

Agenda Preview

Web Brainstorming: *What I need to be aware of transforming power in every moment is…*

Personal Transformation: *Experimenting with transforming power in daily life*

Light & Lively

Empathy: *Feedback*

Journaling: *Experimenting with transforming power in daily life*

Reflection

Closing

Gathering for Silence
Change & Write

Gather as a group sitting in a circle. Settle into the silence. After three or more minutes, read the first three points on the poster in a soft, even voice, leave a long pause, then read the next two points:

- ***Stop,*** *sit silently and let yourself fall away. Let what you want, like or understand fall away.*
- ***Open*** *to transforming power. Value all life, the source of your breath, and the source of your heart beat.*
- ***This is enough;*** *nothing you can say or do will make you any more valuable than you are right now.*
- ***Listen*** *for truths working in you, listen to your conscience.*
- ***Speak****, simply and briefly, if there are implications for others.*

Then continue to read the two points below with long pauses. Pace your reading by attempting to hear and absorb the points yourself.

- ***Change*** *by yielding to the implications for your own life.*
- ***Write*** *implications for your life or community in your journal.*
- ***Leave silence*** between speakers; speak only once, if at all.

Stay in silence for at least 10–15 minutes. Come out of silence with a few words, such as: "*Thank you, friends.*" Then greet people around you by holding the hands of the persons on either side of you or shaking hands with them. Ask if there are any thoughts that arose in the silence that anyone would like to share now. Give people a few minutes if anyone offers to speak. Remind people that they may speak in the silence if they feel the words are important to others. Remind people to take notes in their journal. Close with some group reflection on the activity *(see page 7)*. In addition, ask, *Can you feel how active the silence and stopping may be, rather than escaping, sleeping or collapsing? Can you feel how each step is a part of experimenting? Can you feel how each step changes the next step? Can you do each step fully before going on to the next and go back when you feel a step is missing?*

(10–15 minutes)

Web Brainstorming
Awareness of Transforming Power

Once we are aware of our experience of life's transforming power in all times, the easy and the hard, and recognize that this power exceeds all human capacities for destruction or industry, then we are prepared to experiment with transforming power and discernment in our lives, moment to moment and decision to decision. The first step in the experiment is learning how to keep this awareness alert at all times.

Post on the wall:

What I need to be aware of transforming power in every moment is…

Ask people to brainstorm in their journals a list of critical things that help them be aware of transforming power in and around them, and in every person, thing and situation. Remind people that the focus is not on everything one can do, but on what is <u>necessary</u> to keep one's awareness of transforming power alert. Then list things that obstruct that awareness. When finished, find two other people who are finished and as a group write each idea on an index card with a black marker, including all ideas, but no duplicates. Follow these examples (post on wall or board):

ONE IDEA TO A CARD	***USE BIG, BOLD LETTERS***	***FEW WORDS / PHRASES ONLY***

People may write longer statements with pen on the backs of their cards. Then, ask each group of three for one card that seems most important. Read the cards as you post them on the wall or board, grouping similar cards together and different cards separately. Then ask the groups for one more card, using descriptors that apply such as: what is going to be the most challenging, hardest to remember, riskiest, easiest and so forth. Then ask for any that are not up already; discard duplicates. Create names for the groups of cards and relationships among them, if time and interest allow. Stand back and look at what is posted on the wall. Take 10 - 15 minutes at the end of the activity to make notes in your journal. Then reflect on the activity as a group. *(45-60 minutes)*

NOTE: Time requires choosing between ***Web Brainstorming*** and ***Personal Transformation*** or doing one in a cursory manner. *(10-15 minutes)*

Personal Transformation
Experimenting

We need to be changed by experimenting with the power of love and truth in our own lives before we invite others to change. As we increase our awareness of the power of life in every moment, the next key practice is to experiment with that power to shape the everyday activities and artifacts of our lives—to shape our outward life to reflect our inward experience. A conscientious life is not an extraordinary endeavor; rather, it is valuing and having confidence in the ordinary. Integrity is the measure of this experiment, wherein we order what we do and do not do by what is consistent with the nature and flow of transforming power as directed by conscience, compassion and insight.

Integrity

When word, deed and manner are consistent with:

Apparent reality: honest and reliable.

Our true selves: authentic and genuine.

Life's transforming power: valid and fruitful.

Post four headers: <u>Speaking</u>; <u>Action</u>; <u>Time</u>; <u>Work</u>. Brainstorm in your journal for 5–10 minutes about changes you could make in your life and manners in each area to expand your experience of transforming power:

1. ***Speaking**, words, patterns of speech*
2. ***Actions**, attitudes, gestures*
3. ***Time**, ways of managing and using*
4. ***Work**, what to do or stop doing*

Does your manner in each of these areas reflect your confidence in transforming power? How would you change personally in each of these areas if you allowed transforming power to change you?

Split into small groups of 3-4 people. Give each group four sheets, one for each area. Have each group list the ideas they'd like to share, sorted onto the appropriate four sheets. People may make notes for themselves in their journal. Each group reads their four lists as they post them under the appropriate header on the wall. Reflect in the large group. *(45-60 minutes)*

Empathy
Feedback

Empathy is cultivated, not innate, and as such requires practice. Sympathy is the capacity to 'feel with' another person; empathy is the capacity to 'be aware of' another person's feelings. A good companion does not take on emotional contagion, but stays calm, relaxed and non-anxious and so has the cognitive ability to be aware and empathize. We then realize we cannot know what is right or best for another person, but can only imagine how we might face something ourselves and respect the other person's capabilities to face things themselves. This practice in noticing what is going on in ourselves as we listen to another person dramatically changes the way we respond or give feedback to another person. Divide into groups of four people (three works, but not as nicely, and five works well, but takes a lot of time). Post on the wall:

A problem I will face when I live my life based on transforming power in every moment is…

While all writing in the same direction on the paper, ask everyone to copy this stem sentence and complete the sentence. When they are done writing, have them fold the papers into quarters and drop them into the center of their group. Mix the papers up and have each person take one. Repeat this until everyone has a problem that is not their own. Begin by having one person read the problem on her paper as if it is true for herself. Say, "Imagine that somehow life is at a point that this is true for you."

Describe what it is like in your life and the steps you will take to face it.

Have the reader hand the paper to the person to the right, who says, "I have that problem too," and then reads the problem from the paper. Continue until everyone has said, "I have that problem too," reading the paper and responding. Then the second person reads the second problem, responds and passes it to the right until everyone has responded to the second problem and so forth, until all the problems have been addressed by all the participants. Come back to the large group for reflection. Ask: *Was it hard to imagine being in someone else's shoes? Did others describe what your problem felt like better than you could yourself? What is the difference between empathizing and advising?*

(45-60 minutes)

Session V
Feedback

Gathering for Silence:
Available & Prepared

Opening: *Name and a person who loves me and why…*

Agenda Preview

Fishbowl:
Feedback on experimenting with transforming power

Light & Lively
(one with movement and laughter)

Visiting Companions: *Feedback*

Gathering for Feedback

Journaling:
Being a good companion, listening to where words come from…

Reflection

Closing

Gathering for Silence
Available & Prepared

Sitting in the large group before settling into silence, note that in the silence one might reflect on whether or not one is available and prepared by asking oneself these questions (posted on the wall):

Available & Prepared: Questions in Silence

Am I taking care of myself, with enough health, sleep, water, food, activity, curiosity, tranquility and balance to be prepared & available each day?

Is distress intruding that needs to be discharged and reevaluated?

Is my heart open? ...is there grief, fear, anger, apathy, joy, delight, gratitude?

Is my mind open? ...is there confusion, insight, understanding, integrity?

Is my conscience open? ... am I listening, experimenting, changing?

Settle into the silence. After a few minutes, read the points on the Gathering for Silence poster in a soft, even voice as a reminder (pp 32 & 42).

- ***Stop,** sit silently and let yourself fall away. Let what you want, like or understand fall away.*
- ***Open** to transforming power. Value all life, the source of your breath, and the source of your heart beat.*
- ***This is enough;** nothing you can say or do will make you any more valuable than you are right now.*
- ***Listen** for truths working in you and to your conscience.*
- ***Speak,** simply and briefly, if there are implications for others.*
- ***Change** by yielding to the implications for your own life.*
- ***Write** implications for your life or community in your journal.*

Sit in silence for 10–15 minutes. Come out of silence with a few words, such as: "*Thank you, friends.*" Then greet people around you by holding the hands of the person on either side or shaking hands. Ask if there are any thoughts to share. Remind people to take notes in their journals on their own. Close with a reflection *(see page 7)*. *(15–20 minutes)*

Fishbowl
Feedback on Experimenting

At the beginning of the workshop we noted that when one is inwardly guided the line between inspired and distressed may be distinguished by two factors: first, by one's ability to stop, which is why practicing silence is important; second, by one's responsiveness to external feedback, which is why we practice learning to give and receive feedback.

Ask if anyone has *"something you feel clear about that you would like to share and test with the group."* At this point there is usually a pronounced uneasiness with verbal expressions of confusion, requests for clarification, facial expressions of consternation, and questions such as: "What are you talking about?" Just stay relaxed and be a good companion. Anxiety and avoidance are natural responses to the idea of giving and receiving feedback, especially since for most participants feedback has been neglected and unfamiliar at best and at worst punished or a social taboo. People need to be clear about what is being asked of them, but trying it is totally different from talking about it. So often the best thing to do is to try it first and ask questions later, as long as people are feeling relatively safe in their groups.

If someone volunteers, ask him or her to step into the circle and invite his or her companion(s) from earlier to step into the circle, while others sit around the outside circle and watch. If the person has been working in a pair, ask him or her to select one other pair or a couple other people to form a group of four in the circle.

If no one volunteers, clarify that this is "*any of the things you have identified that you personally need to have or need to let go of in order to stay aware of transforming power, truths working within you, or ways in which you are being changed.*"

In the center of the circle have a writing surface: black board, white board, or paper 48cm x 80cm or 18" x 24". Explain that the group typically records affirmed statements in a group journal, but here we will write on a big board or paper so everyone may see the recording process.

Remind the members of the group that their job is to ignore whether or not they like, agree with or understand the statement brought forward. Their job is to pay attention to whether or not they sense the power and life in it, that it rings true or that the words come from conscience or transforming power.

Ask the person to read what he or she is clear about, without elaboration. Then ask each of the other three group members in turn to state whether or not he or she affirms that the statement rings true. If so, go on to the next person. If not, simply ask the listener to tell the speaker, "I don't feel it yet." Typically the speaker replies. Ask him or her not to explain, persuade or defend, but rather to try and connect with and express the sense of transforming power in it. When the whole group affirms a sense of transforming power present, then they record it, both in the person's journal and in the group's journal with the person's name and words used at that time.

If two or three group members do not sense it, then ask the person to give it more attention and bring it back at a later time. If only one person in the group does not sense it, then the other two group members may decide either to refer it back for more attention or to affirm and record it, depending on their sense of where the hesitancy is coming from. If it seems like the person who does not feel it is well-grounded or in touch with the transforming power in life, then the statement should be given more time, but if that person is not well-grounded or in touch with transforming power, then the group's obligation is to say so, affirm the statement and record it. Questioning is a consideration granted by the group based on its discernment, not a right of each individual.

Stay mindful of supporting and encouraging insight on the part of the speaker, rather than focusing on 'getting it right' or 'figuring it out'. Practice your ability to sense transforming power in the real, ordinary details of life. Do not mistake passion, uniqueness or a particular appearance for transforming power. Sensing transforming power is about drawing on all of our human faculties at once—our mind, heart, conscience and senses—to gain our best sense of the real life in a person, time, place and situation, not about applying theories or notions.

Once something is written, take a moment to honor it. Do not rush. Notice the significant accomplishment of a group affirming something as true and significant in one's life. Rushing past this moment may lose it. These statements are then ready to bring forward to read to the whole community for feedback and recording, if or when affirmed.

Briefly go around the circle and ask if the statement is true for anyone else. Do not belabor it; this is not the time to test others on this matter, but rather to notice and affirm, if, by chance, it is true for anyone else or for the whole group. If it's true for others, acknowledge so verbally and add name(s) to the beginning of the statement: "Jesse Joe, Jane Julie and Jason Joshua find that…". If it is true for the whole group, then change the language to 'we' and put everyone in the names of the people in the group to the end of the statement. You may do one to three rounds in the fishbowl, depending on time. Each group is very different.

Preferably this activity is facilitated by someone who is actually experimenting, giving and receiving feedback and recording what is affirmed on a regular basis. This is an activity where practice matters; it's not just about getting the steps or instructions right. Like any art, sport or performance, you will notice the quality of those with special gifts for it and/or those who have investments of time in the practice of it. This is not just about being smart or knowing how.

After everyone has observed one to three cases in the fishbowl, then let people know the next activity will be to practice in their companion groups. Ask if there are any questions before doing this in their pairs or small groups. They may want to go directly to practicing with their companion(s), or they may wish to reflect on the Fishbowl and do a Light & Lively first. At this juncture, it is good to have 2 - 3 people noticing the mood, energy and needs of the group. Reflect on the activity in the large group. Begin with the typical open-ended questions, but you may wish to add: *At the beginning of this activity, what were you feeling? Are you still feeling that way or has that feeling changed?* You may help the group notice how much less fear, anxiety and avoidance there is now than at the beginning and how curiosity, enthusiasm and caring have often replaced the early feelings of anxiety.

(60-90 minutes)

Visiting Companions
Feedback

Conscience takes shape through relationships with each other and the earth. We express conscience in community and rely on others in our community for feedback, whether implicitly or explicitly. Learning to give and receive feedback explicitly, however, may greatly strengthen the accuracy and validity of our discernment. To hone the ability to exchange feedback fruitfully, find one or more companions who commit to practicing. When practicing in a pair or group, stay open to any outcome and do not hold on to a particular outcome or become offended by differences in outcome. A change does not mean the original discernment was wrong. Discernment seeks direction in a particular time and context, not ultimate or final judgement.

Return to the companion groups from before. If there are pairs, put two pairs together or ask a facilitator to join a pair, and ask each group of four (or three) to practice what they saw in the Fishbowl exercise. Give each group paper and pen to record statements they affirm. Ask each group to designate who will record and who will keep time for each person in turn. This cannot be rushed. It sometimes happens very quickly and sometimes takes awhile, so you cannot predetermine how much time each person will need or estimate how long it will take.

Advise people to read over the statements they wrote in their journals in order to select ones that feel 'ripe', meaning clear, true, essential and stable. Each person should select a statement that he or she feels is both true and vital to experimenting with transforming power in his or her life moment to moment.

Tell the group to take about 10 minutes to consider their selected statements silently in light of the first five Tests of Discernment, the statement's nature, integrity, source, writing and the experience of other people in other communities who have practiced in the past. If it holds up under the first five tests, then test it with your companions.

Tests of Discernment

- ***Nature:*** *simple, persistent in the silence, often feels petty or nearly impossible.*
- ***Integrity:*** *honesty, authenticity, and consistency among conscience, action, word and reality.*
- ***Source:*** *listening plainly to where words come from; speaking plainly from one's best sense of what rings true.*
- ***Writing:*** *clarity of the writing in the discipline of a journal.*
- ***Experience:*** *documented historically by other communities.*
- ***Feedback:*** *from 1-3 companions and from a community.*
- ***Expression:*** *in writing, art, news, courts, government, law.*
- ***The Fruits:*** *love, joy, peace, strength, compassion and liberty.*

Each person will read one statement to the group in turn and have the group give feedback and record what the group affirms. This may take just a few minutes or longer depending on the items coming forward and the clarity of the speakers and listeners. Monitor each group to try to ensure that everyone gets a turn to bring a statement forward and to receive feedback. Give everyone a defined time frame, potentially scheduling a long break afterwards so groups may finish at different times. Remind people to be quiet, as other groups may still be working. At the time of the break, walk around to remind everyone to break now for 15 minutes, or in the next five minutes to allow at least ten minutes for the break.

Return to the large group for reflection. Have each group read the statements affirmed and reflect on the experience of the group process. Invite participants to post the statements affirmed on the wall. Bring the statements recorded forward to a gathering for feedback, if there is time.

(45–60 minutes, could take up to 90 minutes)

Gathering for Feedback

Gatherings for silence and sharing lead into the Gathering for Feedback, forming an operating ecology of activities, rather than a menu of independent, stand-alone activities.

Sit in a circle. Read the poster, Gathering for Feedback, below. Ask individuals to read statements confirmed by their companion groups. Repeat the practice of feedback as it was done in the companion groups, but this time in the large group. Go very slowly. Notice and address feelings as they arise. Reflect on the experience fully in the large group.

Gathering for Feedback

State • Clarify • Test • Publish

- ***Gather**, in silence.*

Once quiet and open, then:

- ***Read** a statement that you feel clear about from the experiment with transforming power in your life.*
- ***Ask** "Is it clear?" **Clarify**, as needed.*

Once clear, then:

- ***Listen**, not to if you like, agree with or understand it, but for the sense of transforming power and life in it.*
- ***Test**, does it spring forth from conscience or 'ring true'?*

If not, or not yet:

- ***Say so** and let the person respond. If persistently not or not yet, invite the person to take more time with it.*

If yes:

- ***Publish** it in the community's book with the person's name and words, clearly but without interpreting or improving them.*
- ***Ask**, is this true for anyone else? If not, move on. If so, **acknowledge** and add names or use the community's name.*
- ***Leave silence** after recording a statement to honor it, then move to the next statement until all statements are tested.*

(80–90 minutes)

Gathering for Discernment

A Gathering for Discernment is not scheduled in this workshop, because most participants reach their limit of what they can absorb after exchanging feedback. Once the other activities in this workshop become more common and familiar, however, participants may complete the prior activities more quickly and therefore have more time as well as energy to try a Gathering for Discernment.

Essential personal preparation for all community gatherings, but especially noticeable in the discernment gathering, include:

- Inspiration and humility.
- Daily experimentation and journal writing (logging).
- Silence, solitude and self-care.
- Conscience expressed in relation to others and the earth.
- Public expression and record.

Personal investment in these elements prepares us for public life and changes the type of community we form when we come together.

On the foundation of these preparations, the gatherings for silence, sharing and feedback also prepare us for community discernment in astonishing ways that completely change the nature of our collective discernment. Most participants have little experience with the key practices in this workshop. Rather than try to describe or explain effects of the practices here, I invite you to practice and experience them for yourself over time.

Anyone in the community may bring forward a question, suggestion for community direction, or request for settlement of a dispute in a Gathering for Discernment. The group settles into silence, opening to transforming power. Then the convenor reads the question, statement or request and asks if it is clear, fielding any questions of clarification and responses. Then each person listens for and shares her or his best sense of what is true. Name the sense of the group and record the group's discernment, then settle into closing silence.

Gathering for Discernment

State • Question • Seek Direction • Settle Disputes

- ***Gather****, in silence.*
- ***Read*** *a statement or question about a direction or a dispute.*
- ***Ask****, Is it clear?*
- ***Listen for and speak about****, not to if you like, agree with or understand it, but to where you sense transforming power and life in it.*
- ***Speak again****, after listening to everyone, to name your best sense of the group's discernment of what rings true in it.*
- ***Record*** *the direction or settlement.*
- ***Leave silence*** *after each item recorded to honor it.*

A community may schedule the four types of gatherings at four different times or at one time with four distinct phases of a single gathering.

Discernment moves past individual and companion practices to focus on what is right or rings true for us as a community. Since a workshop is not an intact, ongoing community seeking direction or settling disputes, when we practice in a workshop, the focus is on a universal 'we as a people' or sense of humanity. Ask the group to clarify who 'we' is, such as members of a particular neighborhood, region, age group, or culture or as broad as humanity on the planet.

(90 minutes)

Session VI
Wrap-up

Gathering for Silence

Opening: Name and *one thing I'm taking home with me is…*

Agenda Preview

Whisper Circle or Personal Reflection

Light & Lively

Affirmation Posters

Open Questions

Next Steps

Reflection of the Whole

Closing

Whisper Circle

Have tissues handy. People often cry. Pass out one 7cm x 12cm or 3" x 5" piece of paper and a pen to each person. Ask each person to remember a negative message said to him or her in childhood, then to think of its opposite, an antidote or what that child needed to hear. He or she will then write the positive message on the card, legibly, so the card may be read by someone else. Ask people not to write their names on the cards. When you collect the cards, make sure all the cards are legible and positive. If one is not, ask the author to change it.

Divide into two equal groups. If needed to even the groups, ask a facilitator to step out. Have Group One sit in a circle facing in. Dim the lights and ask them to relax and settle into silence.

Have Group Two leave the room, give them the following instructions and role play these actions before reentering the room.

Give two cards to each person in Group Two. Ask them to check that the cards are positive, legible and not their own, then to hold one in each hand. Tell them, later when they enter the room, to stand behind someone in Group One sitting in the circle. Designate one person as a leader. Ask everyone in Group Two to raise his or her left hand. Check to make sure everyone raises the left hand and does not mirror the leader from across the circle. When the leader bends forward to whisper from the card in the left hand into the left ear, everyone standing also bends forward and does the same, and then stands and waits for everyone to finish. Some sentences take longer to read than others, so wait until everyone is finished before proceeding. Let the leader set the pace for when to whisper the sentence on the card in the right hand into the right ear of the person sitting before you. Again, wait until everyone is finished, then follow when the leader moves to the person on the right.

Act out that much and tell them to repeat these actions until everyone gets back to the position where he or she began.

Once everyone in the group can act out these actions outside the room, enter the room quietly and calmly as a group. Stand behind someone and follow the leader. When the first group has finished going around the circle, pause for a minute or two quietly. Do not switch too fast. Give people in the circle time to feel what that was like. Then ask the people standing to hand the cards to the person in front of him or her and switch places. Repeat the activity, then collect the cards. Then slowly return to the large group to reflect on this exercise.

(40 minutes)

Personal Reflection

Personal Reflection may be done instead of the ***Whisper Circle*** to help each of us reflect on what we have done here, what it means in our lives and what we need to take it home. Post five questions on the wall:

1. What are my strengths that will help me in experimenting with transforming power moment to moment?
2. How will living out my commitment to myself change me? What kind of person will it make me?
3. What might get in the way or be hard in experimenting with transforming power moment to moment?
4. What help do I need, from whom will I ask for help and how?
5. What can I promise myself to do so that I may grow, use my strengths and become who I want to be?

Ask participants to read the questions aloud to the group. Ask people to get out their journals and pens, read their commitments to themselves, write these questions in their own words in their journals, and then take about 20 minutes to answer these five questions (approximately four minutes for each question). The group may or may not reflect in small groups of 3-5 or in companion groups to discuss what doing this activity felt like. One does not have to share the contents of what was written, just how it felt to reflect and write on these questions. Return to the large group to reflect on the exercise together.

(40 minutes)

Affirmation Posters

Make available a large sheet of paper for each person, approximately 30cm x 41cm or 12" x 16". Prepare a sheet with your adjective and name colorfully drawn. Ask each person to do the same, then write a concrete affirmation for each person on that person's sheet of paper. We sometimes draw posters on the last evening and let people write the affirmations in the evening, morning or break. Give session time to finish up. Consider doing one for a cook, sponsor or other major supporter. The group may or may not reflect on this activity at the end.

(20-30 minutes or longer)

Open Questions

Title a board ***Open Questions*** and place chalk or a marker nearby. In the Opening Talk, invite anyone to write ***Open Questions*** on the board as the workshop progresses and address all posted questions in the final session. This gives people time to find their own answers through the activities. Answering remaining open questions can take 5-60 minutes in the last session and may combine with Next Steps. Do not give lengthy expert answers; invite discussion among the whole group. If participants have specialized questions or seek expert advice, consider scheduling a talk by an expert or referring people to readings. This workshop is to learn what we can from the activities and the group.

(5–60 minutes)

Next Steps

Write on a board or paper upcoming events and steps for further training, with clear dates, times, places and topics, including workshops and refresher gatherings along with any other opportunities. Let people know the steps they can take to continue training, become an apprentice on a team or become a facilitator. Explain that this is a volunteer network and that community training is available when enough of us take the responsibility to make it happen.

(10-15 minutes)

Reflection of the Whole

Reflection of the whole takes a moment to step back, look at all the agendas on the wall, notice the overall flow of the workshop and recall what we did and what we learned. Recall helps to imprint learning, leading to greater retention. It is also an opportunity for participants to make comments and discuss their experience with one another. To empower participants, it is advisable for facilitators not to speak during the reflection. Experiment with different ways to get feedback. Pass out small pieces of paper and pens and invite everyone to write a message telling others something important about his or her experience in this workshop.

(20-30 minutes)

Appendices

Moving

Journaling

Visiting

Gathering

Experimenting

Shifting Approach

Author's Note

Bibliography

Moving

Workshop facilitators need a tool box full of games, ice breakers, mood changers and refreshers to assist groups in making transitions, keeping the energy up and maintaining group cohesion. These are not elaborated in this manual. See AVP manuals for cooperative games.

Many of the main activities in this discernment workshop are reflective and verbal. The workshop greatly benefits from including ample physical activity, cooperative cooking, cleaning walking, playing games outdoors or stretching, exercising or working out.

There are several ways to maintain physical balance within the workshop:

- Allow people to spread out, go outside and use more space for doing individual or small group activities. Ring a bell to bring people back.
- Use frequent, short stretch breaks. Do short group stretching before a break or offer 3-5 minutes of optional group stretching on breaks to those who choose to join.
- Use frequent, short Light & Livelies with a lot of movement and/or laughter, such as: Big Wind Blows, Equidistant, Sun and Umbrella, Touch Blue, Jail Break, Octopus, Whoosh, Bump Tag, Pantomime and so forth.
- Integrate other daily activities into the flow of the workshop: cooking, gardening, walking, working projects and so forth.
- Have simple games and handicrafts around to help people enjoy each other's company on the breaks without relying entirely on conversation. Examples are: origami paper with instructions to fold cranes, painting supplies, blocks, art supplies, picture books, jump ropes, bubbles, sidewalk chalk, hop scotch, math puzzles, musical instruments, song books and so forth.

Enjoy one another's company, be active and lively!

Journaling

A journal or log is critical for any sound experiment. A log requires short, disciplined entries; long prose for self-discovery is a different use of a journal. As a rule of thumb, if you want something in your life, do it for ten minutes a week. You may always spend more time, but ten minutes regularly is valuable. Experiment with ways to organize your journal. Remember however that the journal's value is in how well it helps track and support the experiment with transforming power in daily life. People may bring their own journals. Nice journals or blank books may be available for sale. But have on hand make-shift journals: fold three or four sheets of A5 or letter paper in half together and put three staples along the fold. Use a sheet of colored paper on the outside as a cover.

Domains for Journaling may include:

- ***Open Questions:*** During or after the opening talk, distribute journals and suggest people start a page for open questions, which are useful in fueling and directing an experiment. Questions along the way mark progress and remind us of the process of learning.
- ***Cooperative Agreements:*** It is good to write short stories about how each particular cooperative agreement plays out in your life. You might also write about why one is important, difficult or risky, or about questions, concerns or suggestions for the agreements.
- ***Affirmative Vocabulary:*** The power of positive words is hard to fully appreciate. Cultivate detailed, rich expression by writing definitions and reflections on interesting affirmative words, describing things and feelings, giving concrete affirmations and feedback, and so forth.
- ***Commitment to Self:*** Record commitments to oneself in one's journal. See if they change over time, or not.
- ***Expressions of 'True Self':*** Write to get to know oneself, listen to one's body, mind, heart and conscience, get to know one's gifts and talents and become one's authentic, perfect part of the perfect whole. Each of these contributes to practicing integrity and discernment.

- *Experiences of Transforming Power:* When describing experiences of transforming power, one tends to think of the good times when all is well or the 'mountaintop' experiences. It is also good to reflect on experiences of transforming power in hard times when one falls short, is broken, is inadequate or is the perpetrator.
- *Distresses to Release:* In order to be fully alert to transforming power, we need to notice how historic distresses intrude, learn how to discharge them and reevaluate with a clear mind.
- *Experimenting with Transforming Power:* Record what you need to have or let go of in order to stay aware of transforming power in every moment. Note the percentage of the day your awareness is alert. Write about what is on your conscience, how love and truth are working, what it implies for yourself, community or society, and how you are being shaped and changed.
- *Reflections in the Silence:* After personal or group silence, open your journal for a moment to see what insights you might record and the implications for yourself or others.
- *Insights from Reading:* Record the references for what you read along with inspiring and guiding quotes and your reflections. Test the insights and guidance from your experience against the experiences and practices of other individuals and communities who have taken on this commitment to experiment with their lives.
- *Help Needed, From Whom, By Doing What:* Having agreed to give and receive help, especially for healing, feedback and engaging conscience, take notes on your needs and the needs of others who can help you and how. Keep it simple.
- *Feedback:* Writing provides discipline. Before asking for feedback, try to write what you feel is clear in preparation. Write the feedback received and/or the statements that are affirmed by the group.
- *Fruits of the Experiment:* We leave the results or outcomes to the natural consequences of doing the right thing, and trust the fruits of our lives will be love, truth telling, joy, peace, strength, compassion, beauty, truth, equality, liberty, and more. Record how you are using what you need and how you are sharing the rest.

Visiting

Visiting is spending time with someone without any particular agenda or demand in such a way as to get to know one another.

Visiting Oneself is an unusual, yet helpful, concept and an amazing experience. Caring for, listening to and being oneself is also essential for paying attention to and experimenting with conscience or transforming power in daily life. Set time aside to get to know yourself through: ***silence, solitude, reflection, counseling, self-care, self-soothing, listening, learning, recreation, relaxation and personal exploration.***

Discernment is being inwardly guided by one's best sense of what is right and true. Inward direction may guide us, but also may easily lead us astray, proving to be problematic or self-indulgent. Some traditions use self-denial to attempt to control egotism or inward distresses. Although self-denial may keep one from temptations, it does not reveal the genuine self where transforming power resides. Visiting and getting to know oneself is essential. Also, as the population lives to older ages, unresolved internal distresses increasingly intrude. Discernment requires a purity of heart achieved by being burnt clean by honesty rather than by being innocent or denying oneself.

Questions for Being Available & Prepared

- *Am I taking care of myself–health, sleep, water, food, activity, tranquility, balance–to be prepared & available each day?*
- *Is distress intruding that needs to be discharged and reevaluated?*
- *Is my heart open? ...is there grief, fear, anger, apathy, joy?*
- *Is my mind open? ...is there insight, understanding, integrity?*
- *Is my conscience open? ...do I listen, experiment, change?*

Visiting Companions are two to six people who are mutually engaged in this experiment. You may begin with two and over time you may find other people to join you. Follow the steps and address the questions below.

Communities that value discernment share nearly all the same tests of discernment, but what has allowed those communities to operate successfully based on discernment are the abilities to: 1) stop, and 2) exchange feedback. Therefore visiting, getting to know and exchanging feedback with others who are engaged in this same experiment are all essential.

Visiting Companions

- 2-4 people meet routinely (every 1-6 weeks) for 1-3 hours.
- Open with 5-10 minutes of silence.
- Share available time, taking turns equally among the people.
- Pay attention to support emotional release and speech.
- Ask questions that may help, not to discuss, to fill silence or to pursue your own curiosity.
- If asked, repeat what you heard as closely as possible in your companion's words without changing, improving or interpreting.
- Close with 5-10 minutes of silence.

Questions for Visiting Companions

- *How do I experience transforming power in easy and hard times?*
- *What do I need to have or let go of to stay aware of transforming power in every moment?*
- *What truth is working in me? What are its implications?*
- *What am I learning from transforming power? ...is it for others?*
- *How are love and truth prospering in my life? What are the fruits of my experiment, for example: love, joy, peace, strength, compassion, beauty, truth, equality and liberty?*
- *How can I ask for the help that I need?*
- *How can I share the extra that I have?*

Gathering

Companion groups gather to form a community, which in turn stops, listens, shares, exchanges feedback, seeks direction and documents discernment.

Gathering for Silence

Stop • Open • Listen • Speak • Change • Write

- ***Stop**, sit silently and let yourself fall away. Let what you want, like or understand fall away.*
- ***Open** to transforming power. Value all life, the source of your breath and the source of your heart beat.*

***This is enough**; nothing you can say or do will make you any more valuable than you are right now.*

- ***Listen** for truths working in you; listen to your conscience.*
- ***Speak**, simply and briefly, if there are implications for others.*
- ***Change** by yielding to the implications for your own life.*
- ***Write** implications for your life or community in your journal.*

- ***Leave silence** between speakers; speak only once, if at all.*

Gathering for Sharing

Question • Advice • Direction • Dispute

- ***Gather**, in silence and open to transforming power.*

Once quiet and open, then the convenor:

- ***Reads** a question, advice, direction or dispute to the group.*
- ***Asks** "Is it clear?" and clarifies as needed.*

Once clear, then:

- ***Speak** from one's conscience or best sense of what is true.*
- ***Leave silence** between speakers, giving everyone a chance to speak once before speaking again.*
- ***Listen** with empathy, open to becoming personally changed.*

Once insights or themes emerge (repeating with no new ideas):

- ***Speak** again of one's sense of the group as a whole.*
- ***Record** collective insights or implications for later feedback.*

Community documentation, in turn, serves to shape and guide the lives of individuals. This self-referential cycle of input forms an ecology of practice.

Gathering for Feedback

State • Clarify • Test • Publish

- ***Gather****, in silence.*

Once quiet and open, then:

- ***Read*** *a statement that you feel clear about from the experiment with transforming power in your life.*
- ***Ask*** *"Is it clear?"* ***Clarify****, as needed.*

Once clear, then:

- ***Listen,*** *not to if you like, agree with or understand it, but for the sense of transforming power and life in it.*
- ***Test****, does it spring forth from conscience or ring true?*

If not, or not yet:

- ***Say so*** *and let the person respond. If persistently not or not yet, invite the person to take more time with it.*

If yes:

- ***Publish*** *it in the community's book with the person's name and words, clearly but without interpreting or improving them.*
- ***Ask****, is this true for anyone else? If not, move on. If so, acknowledge and add names or use the community's name.*
- ***Leave silence*** *after recording a statement to honor it, then move to the next statement until all statements are tested.*

Gathering for Discernment

State • Question • Seek Direction • Settle Disputes

- ***Gather****, in silence.*
- ***Read*** *a statement or question about a direction or dispute.*
- ***Ask****, Is it clear?*
- ***Listen,*** *not to if you like, agree with or understand it, but to if you sense the transforming power and life in it.*
- ***Record*** *the direction or settlement.*
- ***Leave silence*** *after each item recorded to honor it.*

Experimenting

Experimenting Moment-to-Moment

1. In your own words, write a commitment to experiment with the spirit, power and wisdom of life moment to moment.
2. Experiment with transforming power in daily life:
   - Stay aware of life's power in every moment, in easy and hard times.
   - Stop, let go, open and listen in personal and group silence.
   - Shape daily life to stay aware of and reflect transforming power.
   - Change according to insights and what rings true; trust yourself.
   - Study others who have tried to do the same.
   - Test discernment by its nature, integrity, source, writing, history, feedback from companions and community, expression and fruits.
   - Document queries, insights, practices, direction and mistakes.
3. Write in a journal to log the experiment:
   - Open questions, cooperative agreements, affirmative vocabulary.
   - Commitments to self and expressions of true self.
   - Experiences in easy and hard times and distresses to release.
   - What you need to have or let go of.
   - What conscience, love or truth would say.
   - How you are shaped and changed.
   - Errors or mistakes and reflections from the silence.
   - Insights from reading.
   - Help needed, from whom and by doing what.
   - Fruits of the experiment.
4. Take time with a companion or small group to be silent, stop, open up to power and wisdom, release pain and distress, listen, learn, speak, exchange feedback, allow it to change us and record.
5. Take time in community to be silent, stop, open up to power and wisdom, listen for/to messages, learn, speak, exchange feedback and allow it to change us and record queries, insights, practices, directions and dispute settlements.
6. Publish results of the experiment in news, writing, art, law or court.
7. Live… fully and enthusiastically, with love, truth, justice and mercy.

Shifting Approach

Before facilitating a training in discernment, take a moment to notice some shifts in approach critical to the work:

- ***Sovereignty of state to sovereignty of natural persons:*** the civil rights, women's rights and peace activists who founded the Alternatives to Violence Project acted based on a strong sense of the inherent sovereignty of natural persons. People extend the power of sovereignty to the state for the peaceful order of law, unless that law violates conscience or faith, in which case the sovereignty of natural persons requires us to act. Discernment draws on the inherent authority of the natural person.

- ***Individuals to communities:*** the Alternatives to Violence Project supports personal rather than system change, but community change occupies a middle ground. Human conscience—*the inward knowledge of right and wrong with a compulsion to do what is right*—exists in relationships among people on the land. This discernment workshop maintains the focus on personal rather than system or institutional change, but also includes discerning 'what is right and true for us as a people', not just as individuals.

- ***'Religious' to 'universal':*** Although discernment, "*the ability to perceive and grasp inner character and relationship of things, especially when obscure, leading to keen insight and judgment,*" appears today primarily in religious contexts, it forms the foundation of conscientious, professional and religious lives. We gain the most from practicing discernment with a wide diversity of people.

- ***Consensus among individuals to discernment as a community:*** consensus directs a community to the first steps—gather, seek clarity, and listen to everyone—and then pursues agreement. In discernment, we seek our best sense of what rings true, not what we find agreeable. I often do not agree with what is true. (If I were Almighty, things would be different!) Instead, for discernment we gather to stop, let go, sense the power of life in the subject, affirm our best sense of what is right and true for each individual and notice when what we affirm rings true for us all.

Such shifts are significant, though often subtle. Discernment employs an ecology of practices from individuals to small groups to the community, creating guidance, in turn, for individuals.

Practicing discernment as a community in some ways it is the most ordinary thing in the world, and in other ways it is surprisingly potent and powerful. "Our deepest fear is not that we are inadequate. Our deepest fear is that we are powerful beyond measure" (Marianne Williamson, 1992). We build confidence in our power by relying on it. Discernment invites all of us to reach down deep and publicly declare what we know to be right and true.

Author's Note

Raised in a rural community of farmers, teachers, woodworkers, artists and Quakers in western New York State, I learned by example to question the integrity of my actions and words as an integral part of what I do and say, rather than to separate questions of integrity as complaints, charges, causes or projects. Every act, consideration, decision and word may be considered in terms of congruency with factuality, authenticity, reality and truth, bit-by-bit and day-by-day.

To keep the practice of discernment on track, I discovered we need to:

1. Focus on what is *necessary*, what I need in order to experiment with transforming power in daily life *with no extra effort.*
2. Recognize that practices of discernment *operate as an ecological whole* rather than a menu from which we may pick and choose.
3. *Simplify the practices*—the experience, the experiment, the journal, mutual companionship, community gatherings and public witness.
4. Recognize the *universality of discernment* for people who share a faith in life whether based on conscience, ethics, spirituality, religion or some combination thereof.

Although I wrote this book in the format of an AVP special topic workshop, which may be used by AVP facilitators and communities, it does not represent the AVP organization. Whether or not this is embraced by AVP remains to be seen and most likely will be appreciated by some and not by others.

Discernment relies on a confidence in the capability and sovereignty of the natural person, with a belief so strong it orders action. Groups of all ages, communities, organizations and businesses who wish to experiment with the transforming power and spirit of life may organize based on integrity, conscience and discernment, if they choose to do so. I look forward to experimenting with, testing and documenting this proposition.

Nadine Hoover, March 2014
Silver Wattle Quaker Centre
Bungendore, NSW Australia

Bibliography

Alternatives to Violence Project, *Manual Basic Course (Revised 2002).* AVP/USA: St. Paul, MN. Order through *http://www.avpusa.org/*

Alternatives to Violence Project, *Manual for Second Level Course (Revised 2005).* AVP/USA: St. Paul, MN. Order through *http://www.avpusa.org/*

Haines, Pamela (2006-present). *Living in this World.* Retrieve at: *http://pamelascolumn.blogspot.com/*

Hoover, Nadine C. with Lee H. Norton and Pamela A. Haines. (2010) *Trauma Healing: Advanced Workshop Manual.* Conscience Studio: Alfred, NY.

Sheeran, Michael J. (1983). *Beyond Majority Rule: Voteless Decisions in the Religious Society of Friends.* Philadelphia Yearly Meeting: Philadelphia: PA.

www.ingramcontent.com/pod-product-compliance
Lightning Source LLC
Chambersburg PA
CBHW031219270326
41931CB00006B/614

9780982849231